Moo p

Mary Murphy

RED FOX

Bye, Moonchap!
Good luck!
We'll miss you!

Moonchap and his friends lived on a tiny crowded island. “We need more space,” said Moonchap one day. “I’ll find a new place to live.”

So he rowed out into the big ocean, looking for a new home.

At last he stopped.

"Perfect!" he said, looking around. "There's plenty of space. I wonder if the people are friendly."

Hello!
Hi!

Two houses stood near the shore. Moonchap went up the neat path to the smart square house and tapped on the door. A square answered straight away.

"I am Moonchap," said Moonchap. "I think I might move here."

"Great!" said the square. "I am Square. Come in and have lunch with me!"

"Thank you," said Moonchap.

Square's home was perfectly tidy.

"Neat as a pin!" said Moonchap.

"Yes," said Square proudly.

He cut squares of cheese for sandwiches. "I like food with straight sides," he said. He sliced eggs, too, perfectly straight. He set the table with square plates and square serviettes. "Time for lunch!" he said.

Moonchap bit a hole in his sandwich. "My sandwich has a mouth!" he said. He made eyes with egg slices. Cheese fell out of his sandwich. Moonchap nibbled it. He even ate the crusts. "Yum!" he said.

Square ate his sandwich carefully, first one half, then the other. He chewed everything twenty times, and didn't speak until he was finished.

"Now," said Square, "I am a square sort of fellow. I always have a nap at this time."

"Wonderful idea," said Moonchap. "I will visit your neighbour."

"My neighbour!" said Square. "Don't bother! Circle is a hopeless, foolish mess!"

"Don't worry, I like all sorts of shapes of people," said Moonchap. "Enjoy your nap!"

He went up the road to Circle's house.

Circle's house had round stones plomped here and there instead of a path.

A ladder went up to the door. Up climbed Moonchap.

The door opened.

"Hello," said Moonchap, "I am . . ."

"Visitors!" said Circle. "Fantastic! Come in!"

In climbed Moonchap.

“Do sit down,” said Circle. “No! I have a better idea. Let’s play ring-a-ring ’o roses.”

They played ring-a-ring ’o roses, hula-hoops, and skipping.

“She’s fun!” thought Moonchap, though he was a bit dizzy with all the circle games.

At last they stopped for a bubbly drink.

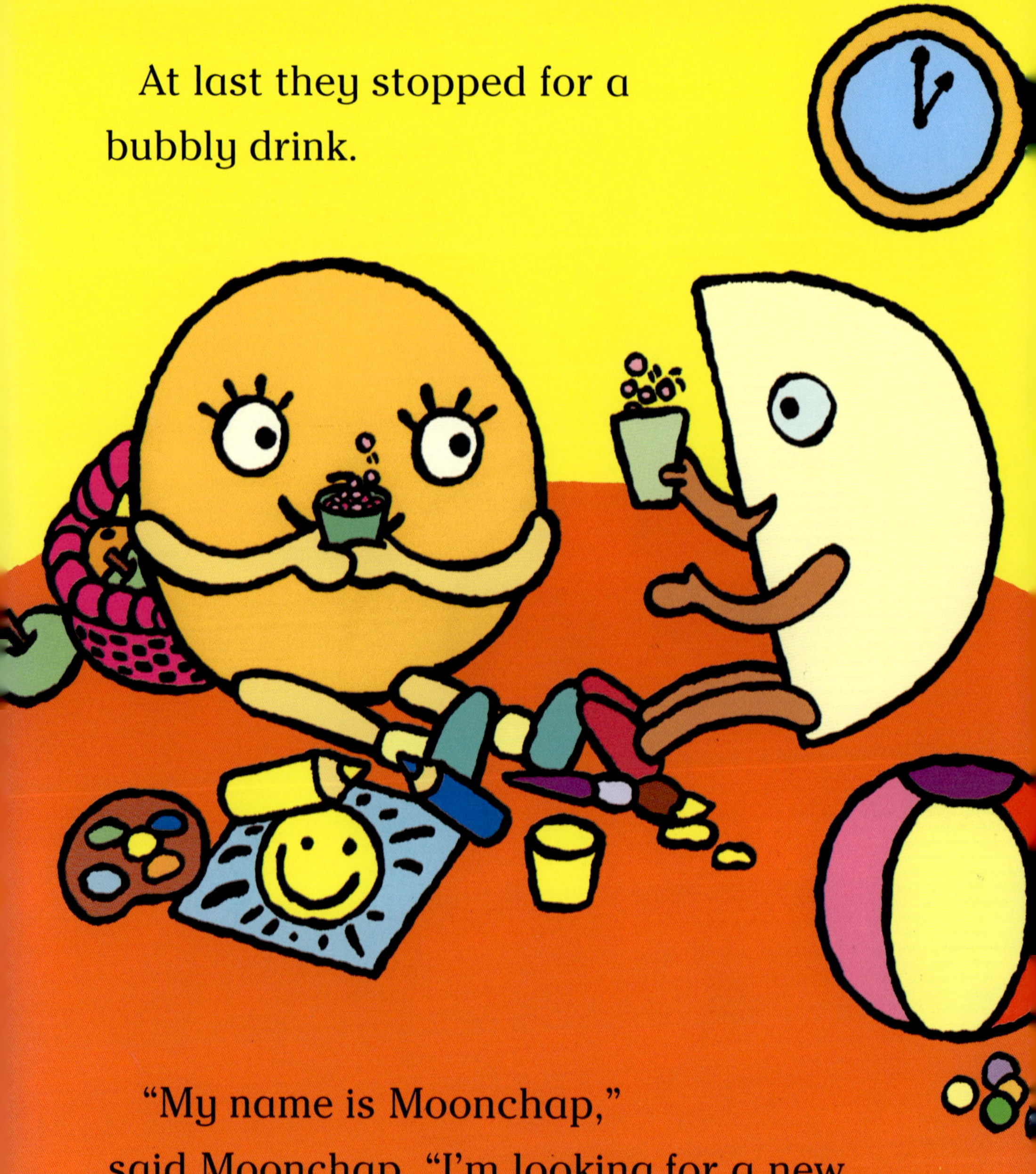

“My name is Moonchap,” said Moonchap. “I’m looking for a new home. Your friend, Square, said—”

“SQUARE!” cried Circle. “He’s not my friend! He’s bossy, he’s a know-all, and he’s no fun!”

“He was kind to me,” said Moonchap.

“Huh!” said Circle.

It was late. Moonchap said goodbye and went back to his boat to sleep.

"I like it here," he thought, "but I wouldn't like it if Circle and Square always fought. I will look for a new home again tomorrow."

In the morning, Moonchap went to say goodbye to Square.

"Don't go!" begged Square. "You are my only friend. You're like me!"

It was true that Moonchap had a straight side like Square. "Well, can we all be friends, you, me and Circle?"

"Well, OK," said Square.

Moonchap went to talk to Circle.

"I only want to stay here if we can all be friends," said Moonchap.

"Please stay!" said Circle. "I like you! You're half like me!"

It was true that Moonchap had a bouncy side like Circle.

"Square will try to be friends," said Moonchap. "Will you?"

"I'll try," said Circle.

Moonchap arranged a picnic to celebrate.

Square was on time. Circle bounced along later. "Here I am!" she cried gaily.

"Typical," muttered Square. "Always late."

"Grumpy!" said Circle.

"Being late is just plain rude," said Square.

"Making personal comments is ruder!" said Circle.

"Now, now," said Moonchap.

But nobody listened.

"Straightsides!" yelled Circle.

"Endless!" roared Square.

"DON'T CALL ME ENDLESS!" screamed Circle, throwing a sandwich at Square.

Square poured lemonade all over Circle.

They kicked and thumped
and pulled and pushed.
Then suddenly . . .

SNAP!

. . . the two shapes broke in half.

Moonchap rushed to his boat for his toolbox to fix Square and Circle.

But he was in such a hurry, he stuck half of Square to half of Circle, and half of Circle to half of Square.

The two new shapes looked at themselves. They looked at each other.

"What are we?" they asked.

"I'm not sure," said Moonchap. "Let me try to fix you."

But the two shapes didn't listen. "We feel strange," they said. They walked away, feeling confused.

Weeks passed. Moonchap worked hard building a house.

At first, the new shapes watched. Then they helped.

At last the house was finished.

Moonchap wrote
a letter to his old
friends, far away.

They wrote back.

"It's a lovely day and my house is finished," said Moonchap. "Let's have another picnic."

This time there was no fighting. The new shapes shared.

"You seem happy," said Moonchap.

"We understand each other now," said one shape.

"We even like each other," said the other shape.

"But really we are a square and a circle," said one shape.

"So that's what we want to be again," said the other.

"And we promise – no more fighting!" they said together.

Moonchap fetched his toolbox. Carefully, he cut the shapes apart.

Then he stuck half of Square to the other half of Square . . .

. . . and half of Circle to the other half of Circle.

"Ah!" said Circle. "I feel like myself again!"

"Me too," said Square.

"It's great to have two new friends," said Circle.

"The more friends the better," said Square.

"Good," said Moonchap, "because look who's arrived at last!"

"My old friends!"

Hello!
Hello!

Can you name the shapes of Moonchap's friends? Which bits are similar? Which bits are different?

How are *your* friends and family alike? Different?

Square and Circle think they are really different from one another. Are they?

Build houses for Moonchap's friends. What will they look like?

1. Start with an empty cardboard box.

2. Cut out the windows and doors. What shapes will they be?

3. Decorate your houses. Think about the shape that lives there to help you decide what each house will look like.

4. Stick on the roof!

YOU WILL NEED: glue, scissors, lolly sticks, coloured card

Make puppet shapes and take them for a visit!

Cut out two bits of card in the same shape. Glue a lolly stick to one shape. Stick the other shape on top. Draw on the faces!

My brothers and sisters

Mary Murphy

How did you get the idea for this story? I wanted to do a story about shapes. As soon as I drew a square and a circle I thought – they might be *very* different, and they might fight. So who would bring them together? Someone who was kind of like a circle and kind of like a square . . .

Which of the shapes do you like most? I think I like Moonchap most, because he is adventurous and helpful, and friendly to everyone.

Is your house like any of the shapes' houses? From the outside, my house is all straight lines, so it's more like Square's home. The inside of my house is more like Circle's home, because it is usually untidy and mixed-up.

What did you use to make the pictures in this book? I used black Indian ink and brushes for the drawing. Then I put the colour in on the computer.